SWEET TO THE SOUL, HEALTH TO THE BONES

DEDICATION

This book is dedicated to my amazing and brilliant wife Michelle. You bring such happiness to my life that even strangers can see it. You truly complete me!

To my children, Kelvin and Destini.
I love you both so very much. This little book is an example of what I taught you as kids; "leave your fingerprints on this earth in a positive way before you leave it."

To Mom. What a great cheerleader and loving supporter you've been all of my life. To say I love you seems to be not enough...

To Damian, Tanya, Nancy, Marcy and Jonetta. Big brother loves you a bunch!

To my pastor, and friend, Bishop Larry Jackson. Without you, there would be no **this**!

CONTENTS

FOREWORD

While driving to church, I felt a strong desire to get the body of Christ to participate in the service more. This should go beyond singing songs and giving of their money. In an instant an idea came that involved the word of God and would enhance something that is common in the church today.

Taking notes during church services has become a regular occurrence in this generation. The problem I've always noticed is that many of the notebooks containing the notes aren't opened and studied during the week. I found that they could lose the understanding that caused the note to be taken in the first place.

It is also very apparent that the body of Christ actually isn't consuming enough of the word of God on their own. There isn't a shortage of teaching and preaching but a lack of personal research and study.

2 Timothy 2:15 **Study to shew thyself approved unto God, a workman that needeth not to be ashamed, rightly dividing the word of truth.**

We are also encouraged by the Christians who heard Paul and Silas at Berea. After they were taught they studied the scripture to see if the things taught aligned with the scriptures and proper doctrine.

*Acts 17:10 **And the brethren immediately sent away Paul and Silas by night unto Berea: who coming** thither **went into the synagogue of the Jews.***

*Acts 17:11 **These were more noble than those in Thessalonica, in that they received the word with all readiness of mind, and searched the scriptures daily, whether those things were so.***

I've used this principle many times to instruct our church to never take anyone's teaching as a blank check, but rather search the scripture for themselves. I'm so thrilled when someone in the right spirit questions me about what I've taught in order to learn or understand more about it. Unfortunately, there is a segment of the church that thinks it is their duty to critique and challenge preaching. But this is the wrong spirit.

I realized during my drive, these problems could be changed by my asking the note takers one simple question. What did you learn today?"

This question instilled a new zeal in note taking in our church. Once this question was asked, hands all over the sanctuary would go up to share what they wrote in their notes. Many times this session would lead into even more explanation concerning a particular point.

Duvale Murchison moved from Lansing, Michigan to Charlotte, North Carolina and was directed to attend Bethel Outreach International Church by one of our mutual close friends. I didn't know him nor did he know me but we both knew Pastor Sean Holland at the Epicenter of Worship in Lansing.

Duvale immediately took to this note taking, "what did you learn?" environment. Many times after church we would discuss what was written in his notes and enjoy the revelation of the message all over again.

In a year and a half, his notebook has become filled with notes that have challenged and given instruction for his life.

When he asked me if it would be okay to publish this book full of these quotes, I was thrilled that someone would consider this undertaking and wholeheartedly gave my consent.

I believe these one sentence sermons will help increase your relationship with the Lord in the way that they have done in many of our lives at Bethel Outreach International Church.

I truly believe that you will enjoy this innovative book and hope that it inspires others to take a more serious look at the notes they take each week while attending a church service.

I hope you enjoy these quotes and apply them to your daily walk with God and His Christ!

Bishop Larry Jackson

INTRODUCTION

This book was inspired by quotes taken from teachings and sermons given by my pastor Bishop Larry Jackson over a 20 month period.

The motivation to put them in book form came during a men's meeting where my pastor's Pastor, Bishop Wellington Boone, spoke.

In the course of the discussion, he said "create your own intellectual properties." These words instantly unfolded a vision within me that lead to the creation of this book.

It is my prayer that at least one of these quotes will inspire you; challenge you; motivate you; move you to a deeper prayer life; increase your meditation and in some special way be as sweet as honey to your soul and health to your bones.

INSPIRATION

Dictionary.Com defines Inspiration as "an inspiring or animating action or influence".

You will find that these simple yet powerful inspiring quotes are calls to action packed with truth and wisdom.

Read, study and meditate on them daily. Allow them to provide spiritual nourishment to your soul and watch the power of God move in your life.

Solomon said it best when he said "Pleasant words are like a honeycomb, sweetness to the soul and health to the bones." (Proverbs 16:24).

"God wants me to produce far more from my gifts than what He initially gave me."

PERSONAL REFLECTIONS

_____
_____
_____
_____
_____
_____
_____
_____
_____

"Jesus has to become greater than anything in my life."

PERSONAL REFLECTIONS

_____
_____
_____
_____
_____
_____
_____
_____
_____

"God celebrates us!"

PERSONAL REFLECTIONS

_____
_____
_____
_____
_____
_____
_____
_____

"What can God invent through me, by me using my gifts and skills?"

PERSONAL REFLECTIONS

_____
_____
_____
_____
_____
_____
_____
_____

5

"When the Holy Spirit comes into our lives, He starts fixing before manifesting."

PERSONAL REFLECTIONS

_____
_____
_____
_____
_____
_____
_____
_____

"When the Holy Spirit opens a door, make sure your fingerprints are not on the handle!"

PERSONAL REFLECTIONS

_____

_____

_____

_____

_____

_____

_____

_____

"One of the goals of God is to bring us to authenticity."

PERSONAL REFLECTIONS

_____
_____
_____
_____
_____
_____
_____
_____
_____

"There's nothing great that hasn't happened without great sacrifice."

PERSONAL REFLECTIONS

_____
_____
_____
_____
_____
_____
_____
_____
_____

9

"Our soul is supposed to be under the rule and control of the Spirit which is complete uninterrupted contact with God."

PERSONAL REFLECTIONS

_____
_____
_____
_____
_____
_____
_____
_____
_____

"The Holy Spirit is the Helper, not the doer."

PERSONAL REFLECTIONS

_____
_____
_____
_____
_____
_____
_____
_____
_____

"People should be able to look at my calendar and find God in it."

PERSONAL REFLECTIONS

_____
_____
_____
_____
_____
_____
_____
_____

"I won't grow as much as I possibly can in my lifetime without connecting with the broader Body of Christ."

PERSONAL REFLECTIONS

_____
_____
_____
_____
_____
_____
_____
_____

"We have to divorce ourselves from options outside of God."

PERSONAL REFLECTIONS

_____
_____
_____
_____
_____
_____
_____
_____

"A good place of power is to enter into someone else's hurt and pain."

PERSONAL REFLECTIONS

_____
_____
_____
_____
_____
_____
_____
_____

"God will give me solutions to impossible problems when I stay under His authority."

PERSONAL REFLECTIONS

_____
_____
_____
_____
_____
_____
_____
_____
_____

"Take care of God's business and He will take care of yours."

PERSONAL REFLECTIONS

_____
_____
_____
_____
_____
_____
_____
_____

"Our words are powerful. Therefore, talk to your life and command it like you would a well-trained dog."

PERSONAL REFLECTIONS

_____
_____
_____
_____
_____
_____
_____
_____

18

"Functioning in the promises of God begins with changing self."

PERSONAL REFLECTIONS

_____
_____
_____
_____
_____
_____
_____
_____

"The more I serve this generation, the greater I become."

PERSONAL REFLECTIONS

_____
_____
_____
_____
_____
_____
_____
_____

"Would God be pleased to make a world full of people who behave like me?"

PERSONAL REFLECTIONS

_____
_____
_____
_____
_____
_____
_____
_____

21

"I need to be a walking revival!"

PERSONAL REFLECTIONS

_____
_____
_____
_____
_____
_____
_____
_____

"Christ not only died FOR me, He died AS me."

PERSONAL REFLECTIONS

_____
_____
_____
_____
_____
_____
_____
_____

23

"God made us kings and priests to run the earth like He wants it ran."

PERSONAL REFLECTIONS

_____
_____
_____
_____
_____
_____
_____
_____

24

"I don't need to ask for grace and favor from God because I already have it."

PERSONAL REFLECTIONS

_____
_____
_____
_____
_____
_____
_____
_____
_____

"The Word of God can either be words on a page or life. Make a choice."

PERSONAL REFLECTIONS

_____
_____
_____
_____
_____
_____
_____
_____

"Stop letting life handle you.
Handle it!"

PERSONAL REFLECTIONS

_____
_____
_____
_____
_____
_____
_____
_____

"Jesus destroyed the works of the devil so that means he's out of business."

PERSONAL REFLECTIONS

_____
_____
_____
_____
_____
_____
_____
_____

"God is using every problem I have in life to get me closer to Him."

PERSONAL REFLECTIONS

_____
_____
_____
_____
_____
_____
_____
_____

"All things are working together for the good of them who love God, even the good and the bad."

PERSONAL REFLECTIONS

_____
_____
_____
_____
_____
_____
_____
_____

"Sin. Let God clean it privately or He is obligated to deal with it openly."

PERSONAL REFLECTIONS

_____
_____
_____
_____
_____
_____
_____
_____

31

"If I don't grow to the level of the assignment predestined for me, I'll always operate below the level of my true abilities."

PERSONAL REFLECTIONS

_____
_____
_____
_____
_____
_____
_____
_____

"God travels at the speed of intent."

PERSONAL REFLECTIONS

_____
_____
_____
_____
_____
_____
_____
_____
_____

33

"Whom I have compassion for; I have the ability to help change."

PERSONAL REFLECTIONS

_____
_____
_____
_____
_____
_____
_____
_____

34

"God wants to do the will He has for us more than we want it."

PERSONAL REFLECTIONS

_____
_____
_____
_____
_____
_____
_____
_____

"Sheep enjoy plenty when they follow the Shepherd. Stay connected."

PERSONAL REFLECTIONS

_____
_____
_____
_____
_____
_____
_____
_____

"Sheep don't listen for the cadence (rhythm) of the Shepherd, they listen for and tune into His frequency."

PERSONAL REFLECTIONS

_____
_____
_____
_____
_____
_____
_____
_____

37

"When we're not flowing or things aren't moving so smoothly, God may be purging us. Therefore, press hard into Him."

PERSONAL REFLECTIONS

_____
_____
_____
_____
_____
_____
_____
_____

"Husbands love your wives. The more she submits, the more you love! She should never be able to out-submit your love."

PERSONAL REFLECTIONS

_____
_____
_____
_____
_____
_____
_____
_____

"The Radical Obedience to God challenge. Who's up for it?"

PERSONAL REFLECTIONS

_____
_____
_____
_____
_____
_____
_____
_____

"God will never move me past the level of my obedience."

PERSONAL REFLECTIONS

_____
_____
_____
_____
_____
_____
_____
_____
_____

"There should be no evidence of the world in me."

PERSONAL REFLECTIONS

_____
_____
_____
_____
_____
_____
_____
_____
_____

FAITH

Of everything Jesus said and did, the miracle of the withered fig tree has mystified me the most. He cursed the tree and within 24 hours, it was dried up at the roots.

The tree withering is not necessarily the big deal for me. It is what Jesus said to Peter when he mentioned how quickly the tree died.

Jesus simply stated, "Have faith in God." (Mark. 11:21-22)

He didn't instruct Peter to do anything special for that type of miracle. Jesus didn't preach a five point sermon. Instead, Jesus gave us all a lesson in practical faith with only four words.

When we ask God for things, our emphasis must be on Him! If our faith is focused more on the manifestation of the *stuff* we ask for then we missed it!

Have faith in GOD!

"Faith is too high to just devote to stuff you want."

PERSONAL REFLECTIONS

_____
_____
_____
_____
_____
_____
_____
_____
_____

44

"There has to be an element of faith before I pray about a thing."

PERSONAL REFLECTIONS

_____
_____
_____
_____
_____
_____
_____
_____
_____

"When the woman with the issue of blood touched Jesus, He basically asked 'who took some of heaven's resources and how did they know how to get it'?"

PERSONAL REFLECTIONS

_____
_____
_____
_____
_____
_____
_____
_____

"Since Jesus gave us His power, how then does hell have power over us?"

PERSONAL REFLECTIONS

_____
_____
_____
_____
_____
_____
_____
_____

"The moment we try to fix a problem turned over to God, that is the moment we cut off and defuse His power."

PERSONAL REFLECTIONS

_____
_____
_____
_____
_____
_____
_____
_____

48

"Assumptions always kill faith."

PERSONAL REFLECTIONS

_____
_____
_____
_____
_____
_____
_____
_____

"How do I know when I'm not presuming and using faith?"

PERSONAL REFLECTIONS

_____
_____
_____
_____
_____
_____
_____
_____
_____

"When I don't see the
HIM-possible,
I will always default to the
Impossible.
Operate on the
HIM-possible
side of the ledger."

PERSONAL REFLECTIONS

_____
_____
_____
_____
_____
_____
_____
_____

51

"The faithless Christian believes as long as s/he feels like they have an option outside of God, they'll take it."

PERSONAL REFLECTIONS

_____
_____
_____
_____
_____
_____
_____
_____

"If I have faith to believe that I'm saved because of a simple prayer, what happened to my faith from that point?"

PERSONAL REFLECTIONS

_____
_____
_____
_____
_____
_____
_____
_____

53

"My mind produces what I believe."

PERSONAL REFLECTIONS

_____
_____
_____
_____
_____
_____
_____
_____

"If I focus on the struggle, I'll walk into unbelief and then start asking unbelief questions."

PERSONAL REFLECTIONS

_____
_____
_____
_____
_____
_____
_____
_____

"Faith grabs what is hoped for in the unseen, makes it substance in the spiritual realm and manifests it in the natural."

PERSONAL REFLECTIONS

_____
_____
_____
_____
_____
_____
_____
_____

"When we are in faith, what happened yesterday doesn't affect my today. When my faith is being tested, it may be God."

PERSONAL REFLECTIONS

_____
_____
_____
_____
_____
_____
_____
_____

57

"Getting our healing or miracle is really as easy as believing, as long as we view it from a Kingdom perspective."

PERSONAL REFLECTIONS

_____
_____
_____
_____
_____
_____
_____
_____

"Get it out of your mind that things must look good as you trust God in the process of something coming together."

PERSONAL REFLECTIONS

_____
_____
_____
_____
_____
_____
_____
_____

"When God? How God? Why God? When we let God be God, we'll lose those questions."

PERSONAL REFLECTIONS

_____
_____
_____
_____
_____
_____
_____
_____
_____

"We can never beat the devil by using his weapons."

PERSONAL REFLECTIONS

_____
_____
_____
_____
_____
_____
_____
_____

"...God, BUT;
...But, GOD!
Is your but
in the wrong place?"

PERSONAL REFLECTIONS

_____
_____
_____
_____
_____
_____
_____
_____

"Hope is the anchor of the soul. It keeps us anchored."

PERSONAL REFLECTIONS

_____
_____
_____
_____
_____
_____
_____
_____

MOTIVATION & SUCCESS

Has is ever dawned on you that God loves you so much that He has *custom made* success with your name on it?

It's like having tailor made victories and triumphs made just for you by the hands of God!

God told Joshua, "This book of the Law shall not depart from your mouth but you shall mediate in it day and night...then you will make your way prosperous and then you will have good success." (Joshua 1:8)

Success! God's way or yours?

"Be a genius in the area of life God places you in."

PERSONAL REFLECTIONS

_____
_____
_____
_____
_____
_____
_____
_____

"Be alert to satanic snipers trying to pick you off."

PERSONAL REFLECTIONS

_____
_____
_____
_____
_____
_____
_____
_____
_____

"If a leader asks me to do something, I must do it under their leadership. I have to then step out of my own leadership position or I will inevitably compete with my leader."

PERSONAL REFLECTIONS

_____
_____
_____
_____
_____
_____
_____
_____

67

"If something doesn't advance me and the Kingdom simultaneously, it's more than likely not from God."

PERSONAL REFLECTIONS

_____
_____
_____
_____
_____
_____
_____
_____

"Bad things will happen in our lives when we take the exit ramp off God's path."

PERSONAL REFLECTIONS

_____
_____
_____
_____
_____
_____
_____
_____

"True leaders have learned through discipline how to make their words and behavior match."

PERSONAL REFLECTIONS

_____
_____
_____
_____
_____
_____
_____
_____
_____

"I don't have to be in a great place to be used for greatness."

PERSONAL REFLECTIONS

_____
_____
_____
_____
_____
_____
_____
_____
_____

"What I am in private will come out publicly."

PERSONAL REFLECTIONS

_____
_____
_____
_____
_____
_____
_____
_____
_____

"Struggles along my path are designed for my greatness."

PERSONAL REFLECTIONS

_____
_____
_____
_____
_____
_____
_____
_____

"God does not know how to create average. We're the ones who think we're average."

PERSONAL REFLECTIONS

_____
_____
_____
_____
_____
_____
_____
_____

"Give God the glory for personal recognitions and compliments and send criticisms *return to sender.*"

PERSONAL REFLECTIONS

_____
_____
_____
_____
_____
_____
_____
_____
_____

75

"If I factor God out of any decision, I have missed the equation."

PERSONAL REFLECTIONS

_____
_____
_____
_____
_____
_____
_____
_____

"We stop dreaming when the level of our dreaming stops at the level of only making money."

PERSONAL REFLECTIONS

_____
_____
_____
_____
_____
_____
_____
_____

77

"Can I live with the same desperation for God when I'm lacking as when I'm balling?"

PERSONAL REFLECTIONS

_____
_____
_____
_____
_____
_____
_____
_____
_____

"If I'm not excelling in my gift sets, that is because I'm not tapping into the *exceedingly abundantly* part of God in my life."

PERSONAL REFLECTIONS

_____

_____

_____

_____

_____

_____

_____

_____

79

"Beware of a man of low character."

PERSONAL REFLECTIONS

_____
_____
_____
_____
_____
_____
_____
_____

"To get to the ultimate level of compassion, I have to cultivate humility."

PERSONAL REFLECTIONS

_____
_____
_____
_____
_____
_____
_____
_____

81

"Are you so comfortable and complacent that there is no innovation in your life?"

PERSONAL REFLECTIONS

_____
_____
_____
_____
_____
_____
_____
_____

"If you don't cause yourself to see *big* and *great*, *little* will have you."

PERSONAL REFLECTIONS

_____
_____
_____
_____
_____
_____
_____
_____
_____

"Never use a person who is not producing."

PERSONAL REFLECTIONS

_____
_____
_____
_____
_____
_____
_____
_____

MEDITATION

Think about how great it feels when someone scratches your back in just the right spot. Oh my! What an awesome thing. Mediation has a way of soothing the soul like that.

King David wrote "…but his delight is in the law of the Lord and in His law he meditates day and night…and whatever he does shall prosper." (Psalms 1:2,3).

Meditate the bible way and watch amazing things inexplicably unfold in your life. (Joshua 1:8)

"We are limited because we think *church* and not *Kingdom.*"

PERSONAL REFLECTIONS

"How do we really know when the Holy Spirit is around?"

PERSONAL REFLECTIONS

_____
_____
_____
_____
_____
_____
_____
_____

"Our spirit can move our emotions but the emotions can't move our spirit."

PERSONAL REFLECTIONS

"Think *Kingdom* and not *earth*."

PERSONAL REFLECTIONS

_____
_____
_____
_____
_____
_____
_____
_____

"Jesus never started at the place of need. He started at the place of Kingdom. Heavenly results come from Kingdom minded people."

PERSONAL REFLECTIONS

"On a scale of 1 - 10, where is my level of compassion?"

PERSONAL REFLECTIONS

_____

_____

_____

_____

_____

_____

_____

"If we know we are kings, why do we think like paupers?"

PERSONAL REFLECTIONS

_____
_____
_____
_____
_____
_____
_____
_____
_____

"If I have a negative internal, emotional reaction to seeing or hearing someone's name that has offended me, I haven't truly forgiven them."

PERSONAL REFLECTIONS

"As a priest of God, you can't have an epidural to the things of life and other people's lives."

PERSONAL REFLECTIONS

_____
_____
_____
_____
_____
_____
_____
_____

94

"True tithe mentality says 'God, how much do you want me to keep'?"

PERSONAL REFLECTIONS

_____
_____
_____
_____
_____
_____
_____
_____
_____

"We must view the world from a biblical perspective and not view the bible from a worldly perspective."

PERSONAL REFLECTIONS

_____
_____
_____
_____
_____
_____
_____
_____

"Most church folks are homosectuals; they only worship and fellowship with their own kind."

PERSONAL REFLECTIONS

_____
_____
_____
_____
_____
_____
_____
_____
_____

"We keep losing battles because we keep fighting against the wrong enemy."

PERSONAL REFLECTIONS

_____
_____
_____
_____
_____
_____
_____
_____

"We struggle in our walk with God because old things have not passed away."

PERSONAL REFLECTIONS

_____
_____
_____
_____
_____
_____
_____
_____
_____

"We hold on to the old man because he's familiar to us and we're comfortable with him."

PERSONAL REFLECTIONS

_____
_____
_____
_____
_____
_____
_____
_____

"I am supposed to be so transformed that I don't even know myself."

PERSONAL REFLECTIONS

_____
_____
_____
_____
_____
_____
_____
_____

"Darkness is attracted to darkness. Light is attracted to light. What darkness in me is Satan attracted to?"

PERSONAL REFLECTIONS

_____
_____
_____
_____
_____
_____
_____
_____

"How much of the world do I like?"

PERSONAL REFLECTIONS

_____
_____
_____
_____
_____
_____
_____
_____

"My life is not about me. It's about the One who brought me here."

PERSONAL REFLECTIONS

_____
_____
_____
_____
_____
_____
_____
_____
_____

"Am I a disciple or just a church-goer?"

PERSONAL REFLECTIONS

_____
_____
_____
_____
_____
_____
_____
_____

"If someone that doesn't know God isn't coming after me to know more about Him, my Godliness is not attractive enough."

PERSONAL REFLECTIONS

_____
_____
_____
_____
_____
_____
_____
_____
_____

"You can't get a whole reward from God with half of a heart."

PERSONAL REFLECTIONS

_____
_____
_____
_____
_____
_____
_____
_____
_____

"Incomplete obedience,
IS disobedience."

PERSONAL REFLECTIONS

_____
_____
_____
_____
_____
_____
_____
_____
_____

"If I don't change the way I think, I'll keep doing and saying the same destructive things."

PERSONAL REFLECTIONS

_____
_____
_____
_____
_____
_____
_____
_____

109

"If I don't know who I am, the world will tell me. I should think highly, but not more highly than I ought to."

PERSONAL REFLECTIONS

_____
_____
_____
_____
_____
_____
_____
_____
_____

"Our behavior is a reflection of the true self concept we have on the inside."

PERSONAL REFLECTIONS

_____
_____
_____
_____
_____
_____
_____
_____

"When we suffer with low self concept, we reduce our behavior down to the level of that understanding."

PERSONAL REFLECTIONS

_____
_____
_____
_____
_____
_____
_____
_____
_____

"Talk to people about Jesus without speaking *Christianese*."

PERSONAL REFLECTIONS

_____

_____

_____

_____

_____

_____

_____

_____

"How do Christian's sin? By choice!"

PERSONAL REFLECTIONS

_____
_____
_____
_____
_____
_____
_____
_____
_____

"When trouble comes like hot water, do we become like sweet tea that's good to drink? Or do we become like a hardboiled egg?"

PERSONAL REFLECTIONS

_____
_____
_____
_____
_____
_____
_____
_____
_____

"I must have a 'fitly joined together' mindset when it comes to the people of God."

PERSONAL REFLECTIONS

_____
_____
_____
_____
_____
_____
_____
_____
_____

"Be the bible tract that you want to hand out."

PERSONAL REFLECTIONS

_____
_____
_____
_____
_____
_____
_____
_____

PRAYER

Prayer, in its simplest form, is talking to God. We don't have to use special rules or formulas to get God's attention. However, unlike talking to people, God hears past our words and looks at what's in our hearts. That's where He begins.

Make it a regular habit to examine your heart before you pray. See if everything measures up in His eyes. When it does, the purity and sincerity of your heart will capture the ear of God in a wonderfully responsive way!

"The eyes of the Lord are on the righteous, and His ears are open to their cry. The righteous cry out, and the Lord hears, and He delivers them out of all their troubles." (Psalms 34:15, 17)

"When we talk to God, we must talk to Him like He is God and (know) He is above our situation."

PERSONAL REFLECTIONS

_____
_____
_____
_____
_____
_____
_____
_____

"We need to step out of time, while still in time, and meet God in prayer."

PERSONAL REFLECTIONS

_____
_____
_____
_____
_____
_____
_____
_____
_____

120

"The level of my resistance to greater fellowship with God must be attacked and overcome by fasting and prayer."

PERSONAL REFLECTIONS

_____
_____
_____
_____
_____
_____
_____
_____

"God turns toward the truly repented heart."

PERSONAL REFLECTIONS

_____
_____
_____
_____
_____
_____
_____
_____
_____

"Pray this; *God, shut off everything that I'm trying to do that is outside of your will and plan for me.*"

PERSONAL REFLECTIONS

_____
_____
_____
_____
_____
_____
_____
_____

123

"As Aaron stood in the gap for the entire nation of Israel, we need to do the same for our entire bloodline."

PERSONAL REFLECTIONS

_____
_____
_____
_____
_____
_____
_____
_____

"Getting changed in prayer is not just what I say, it's what I hear."

PERSONAL REFLECTIONS

_____
_____
_____
_____
_____
_____
_____
_____

"When we're going through a hard time, pray for someone else going through the same thing. That, is our way out."

PERSONAL REFLECTIONS

_____
_____
_____
_____
_____
_____
_____
_____

KNOWING GOD

Can one really get acquainted with God Almighty? Yes! And He wants us to.

There are so many ways to get acquainted with God that none of us will ever live long enough to figure them out. But don't stress out if you feel like your journey to knowing Him feels distant or ineffective. You are certainly not wasting your time. In fact, you are closer than you think!

God tells us to "be still and know that I am God." (Psalms 46:10). The biblical meaning of *still* does not mean be idle. It means to loosen up or relax. To *Know God* means to discover Him by seeing!

So, relax and do your thing! Look for signs of God along your way. That's being still and knowing God!

"God is not into spiritual quickies."

PERSONAL REFLECTIONS

_____
_____
_____
_____
_____
_____
_____
_____
_____

"Do I phileo God or agape God?"

PERSONAL REFLECTIONS

_____
_____
_____
_____
_____
_____
_____
_____
_____

"If everything is IN Christ, why do we look OUTSIDE of Christ for it?"

PERSONAL REFLECTIONS

"Although ALL authority has been given to Jesus, we tend to think there is a competing authority."

PERSONAL REFLECTIONS

_____
_____
_____
_____
_____
_____
_____
_____

"We have the ability to tap into *all knowledge* but we don't because we keep God in our own little church box."

PERSONAL REFLECTIONS

_____
_____
_____
_____
_____
_____
_____
_____

"Is the Holy Spirit just tongues to me?"

PERSONAL REFLECTIONS

_____
_____
_____
_____
_____
_____
_____
_____
_____

"Many of us treat God like an alcoholic husband treats his wife."

PERSONAL REFLECTIONS

_____
_____
_____
_____
_____
_____
_____
_____

"The level of my suffering is commensurate (proportionate) with the level God called me to be."

PERSONAL REFLECTIONS

_____

_____

_____

_____

_____

_____

_____

_____

"When I don't act like the character of God..."

PERSONAL REFLECTIONS

_____
_____
_____
_____
_____
_____
_____
_____

"We speak things out of our mouth and we really don't know how the words are affecting our lives."

PERSONAL REFLECTIONS

_____

_____

_____

_____

_____

_____

_____

_____

"Most of us are living beneath our privileges."

PERSONAL REFLECTIONS

_____
_____
_____
_____
_____
_____
_____
_____

138

"Is my life such that people enjoy being around me?"

PERSONAL REFLECTIONS

_____

_____

_____

_____

_____

_____

_____

_____

"How much are we truly under God's authority and command?"

PERSONAL REFLECTIONS

_____
_____
_____
_____
_____
_____
_____
_____
_____

"How will people know God is really with you?"

PERSONAL REFLECTIONS

_____
_____
_____
_____
_____
_____
_____
_____

"Most of the time we pray like we're trying to know God instead of praying like a true son or daughter."

PERSONAL REFLECTIONS

_____
_____
_____
_____
_____
_____
_____
_____

142

"Most church folks talk about God instead of talking like they just finished talking to and hanging out with Him."

PERSONAL REFLECTIONS

_____
_____
_____
_____
_____
_____
_____
_____

"If we whine and complain while going through a tough season, we have forgotten that we are a child of God."

PERSONAL REFLECTIONS

_____
_____
_____
_____
_____
_____
_____
_____

144

"**Are we truly the high priests of our family and have compassion in the face of their intentional wrong doings?**"

PERSONAL REFLECTIONS

_____

_____

_____

_____

_____

_____

_____

_____

"Is my fellowship with God so close that He comes to me before something bad happens to a member of my family?"

PERSONAL REFLECTIONS

"Tithing shows my obedience to God. Offerings show my love for Him."

PERSONAL REFLECTIONS

_____
_____
_____
_____
_____
_____
_____
_____

"We can't be changed or moved by God if our hearts are attached to worldly things."

PERSONAL REFLECTIONS

_____
_____
_____
_____
_____
_____
_____
_____

"What is standing, sitting or existing between you and God?"

PERSONAL REFLECTIONS

_____
_____
_____
_____
_____
_____
_____
_____
_____

"What gets more of my time than God?"

PERSONAL REFLECTIONS

_____
_____
_____
_____
_____
_____
_____
_____
_____

"Can I truly turn the other cheek?"

PERSONAL REFLECTIONS

"Perfection comes only through suffering."

PERSONAL REFLECTIONS

"You shouldn't hang around God and look too worldly or carnal."

PERSONAL REFLECTIONS

_____
_____
_____
_____
_____
_____
_____
_____

"God doesn't do anything great around anyone's convenience. He does it around sacrifice."

PERSONAL REFLECTIONS

_____
_____
_____
_____
_____
_____
_____
_____
_____

154

"What will God give me, at this very moment, according to my faithfulness?"

PERSONAL REFLECTIONS

_____

_____

_____

_____

_____

_____

_____

_____

_____

"Is God obligated to bless me with wealth if I am not cultivating a relationship with him?"

PERSONAL REFLECTIONS

_____
_____
_____
_____
_____
_____
_____
_____
_____

"In the Kingdom of God, nothing happens outside of relationships."

PERSONAL REFLECTIONS

_____
_____
_____
_____
_____
_____
_____
_____
_____

157

"Are there lines we can cross where God's grace won't sustain us?"

PERSONAL REFLECTIONS

_____
_____
_____
_____
_____
_____
_____
_____

"God loves to wait because the waiting period moves us out of the way."

PERSONAL REFLECTIONS

_____

_____

_____

_____

_____

_____

_____

_____

"Like sheep, we have to be totally dependent on the Shepherd."

PERSONAL REFLECTIONS

"It is the Shepherd's responsibility to lead me, not for me to lead me."

PERSONAL REFLECTIONS

_____
_____
_____
_____
_____
_____
_____
_____
_____

"The Shepherd will defend His sheep. If it doesn't seem that way, perhaps we're trying to defend ourselves and we're not letting the
Shepherd, shepherd."

PERSONAL REFLECTIONS

"Sheep and goats sit together in church. God will eventually get rid of the goats."

PERSONAL REFLECTIONS

_____
_____
_____
_____
_____
_____
_____
_____
_____

"When we're not flowing or things aren't moving so smoothly, God may be purging us. Therefore, press hard into Him."

PERSONAL REFLECTIONS

_____
_____
_____
_____
_____
_____
_____
_____

"Many of us know the rules of driving better than the rules of righteousness."

PERSONAL REFLECTIONS

_____

_____

_____

_____

_____

_____

_____

_____

_____

"Are you talking to the Lord like you have to qualify for His goodness?"

PERSONAL REFLECTIONS

_____
_____
_____
_____
_____
_____
_____
_____

"Jesus is the Good Shepherd. Stop dealing with Him like He's the bad Judge."

PERSONAL REFLECTIONS

Scripture References
NKJV Key Word Study Bible
Pg. 1 Proverbs 16:24
Pleasant words *are like* a honeycomb, Sweetness to the soul and health to the bones.

Pg. 43 Mark 11:21, 22
And Peter, remembering said to Him, "'Rabbi, look! The fig tree which you cursed has withered away." So Jesus answered and said to him, "Have faith in God."

Pg. 64 Joshua 1:8
This Book of the Law shall not depart from your mouth but you shall mediate in it day and night, that you may observe to do according to all that is written in it. For then you will make your way prosperous and then you will have good success.

Pg. 85 Psalms 1:2, 3
Blessed is the man who walks not in the counsel of the ungodly, nor stands in the path of sinners nor sits in the seat of the scornful; but his delight is in the law of the Lord and in His law he meditates day and night.

Pg. 118 Psalms 34:15, 17
For the eyes of the Lord *are* on the righteous, and His ears *are open* to their cry. *The righteous* cry out and the Lord hears and delivers them out of all their troubles.

Pg. 127 Psalms 46:10
Be still and know that I *am* God; I will be exalted among the nations, I will be exalted in the earth!

www.ingramcontent.com/pod-product-compliance
Lightning Source LLC
Chambersburg PA
CBHW060925040426
42445CB00011B/790